Mesi
A GIRL 'n GRACE IN AFRICA

PAM DAVIS

A
Authentic

COLORADO SPRINGS • MILTON KEYNES • HYDERABAD

Authentic Publishing
We welcome your questions and comments.

USA   1820 Jet Stream Drive, Colorado Springs, CO 80921 www.authenticbooks.com
UK   9 Holdom Avenue, Bletchley, Milton Keynes, Bucks, MK1 1QR
       www.authenticmedia.co.uk
India Logos Bhavan, Medchal Road, Jeedimetla Village, Secunderabad 500 055, A.P.

Mesi: A Girl 'n Grace in Africa
ISBN-13: 978-1-934068-51-9
ISBN-10: 1-934068-51-9

Copyright © 2007 by Pam Davis

10 09 08 / 6 5 4 3 2 1

Published in 2008 by Authentic

Scripture quotations are taken from the authorized King James Version. Public domain.

Illustrations: Monica Bucanelli
Cover/interior design: Julia Ryan | www.DesignByJulia.com
Editorial team: Kathy Buchanan, Reagen Reed, Megan Kassebaum
Africa photos: © Galen R. Frysinger (except where noted)
Author photo: © Cliff Ranson, www.ransonphotography.com.
Images: © 2007 iStockphoto.com, © 2007 JupiterImages Corporation

Printed in the United States of America

CONTENTS

WELCOME FROM THE AUTHOR

Introduction of Mesi
Girls 'n Grace Place

In Step with the Times in Africa
Girls 'n Grace Doll Collections

To Alese Chandler Davis, my daughter, with love.

You are forever held in my heart's embrace.
A gift from God, my girl in grace.

Welcome from the Author

Dear friends,

I am so pleased you are joining me as we journey through lives of girls in grace.

A Girl 'n Grace is a girl in whom the person of grace, Jesus Christ, lives. You'll notice there's a missing "I" and an apostrophe in its place. The Bible teaches that in order to live in a relationship with God one must surrender her life to Jesus. No longer do I live but rather it is Christ who lives in me as I live by faith in the Son of God (Galatians 2:20). A Girl 'n Grace is a girl who has surrendered her self-centered desires to the desires of Christ. In doing so, she discovers strength, satisfaction, and significance, which elevates her self-esteem and honors God.

Let this book aid you in discovering the desires of Jesus Christ and may you, like these characters, proclaim, "I can through Christ."®

In his embrace,
Pam Davis
(Acts 20:24)

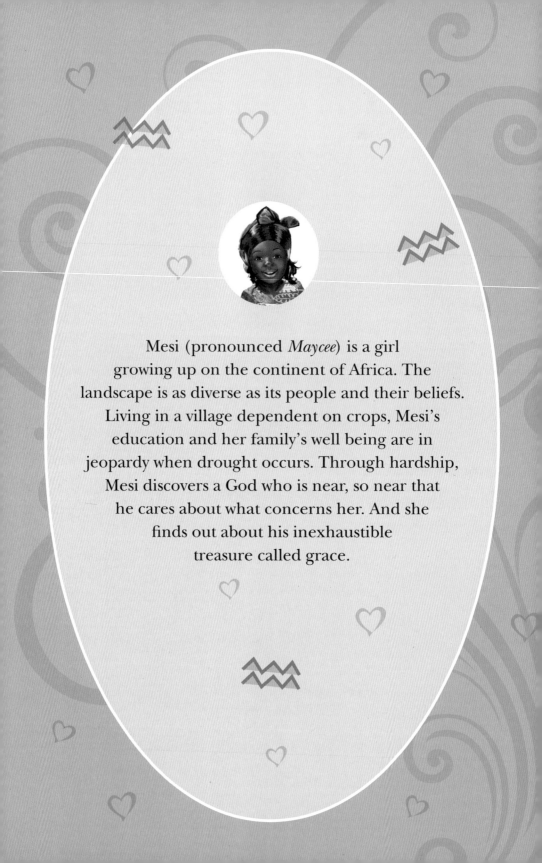

Mesi (pronounced *Maycee*) is a girl
growing up on the continent of Africa. The
landscape is as diverse as its people and their beliefs.
Living in a village dependent on crops, Mesi's
education and her family's well being are in
jeopardy when drought occurs. Through hardship,
Mesi discovers a God who is near, so near that
he cares about what concerns her. And she
finds out about his inexhaustible
treasure called grace.

Girls 'n Grace Place is a fun website where you can interact with the Girls 'n Grace characters. You can. . .

join the free Reader's Club to take a quiz and win a prize! These heart-shaped icons in the book tell you there's a quiz question on the website.

participate with the Girls 'n Grace doll characters through a virtual experience and enjoy a wide range of activities: fashion, reader's club, travel, cooking, decorating, art, education, creating your own Girls 'n Grace magazine, and much more!

Visit the Girls 'n Grace characters at www.girlsngrace.com.

CHAPTER 1

School

Mesi traced the lines of the chain-link fence as she stared through it. She watched groups of students swarm toward the cement-block building, dressed in the school's dark blue uniforms. A lump formed in her throat. She longed to be part of these laughing clusters of children. She'd been able to go for her early years of schooling, but her parents could no longer afford to send her. Uniforms, books, and supplies had to be purchased out of their own pocket, and in a couple of years they'd need to start paying tuition, too. It was just too much—especially with the crops doing poorly this year.

"Besides," her father had told her, "you'll end up as a wife and mother in not too many years. You don't need an education for that. Learn how to make *fufu* and milk a cow." Father was probably right, but she had so much enjoyed school. Secretly, she wanted to be a teacher, but that dream was an impossibility without an education.

"Mesi! Mesi!"

Mesi could recognize the voice anywhere. It was her dear friend—her *chalay*. On the other side of the fence,

Kwasi ran up to her, practically spilling her armful of books everywhere. "What are you doing here?" She touched the tips of Mesi's fingers through the fence.

"Mother sent me to get some water."

Kwasi laughed. "You're a little far from the river, aren't you?"

"I thought I'd take the long route."

Kwasi smiled with understanding. "You wanted to see the school." She tilted her head. "I'm sorry you can't go."

Mesi shrugged as if it didn't matter, even though they both knew it did. "Maybe next year the cocoa crops will be better. There's certainly no money this year for me to go."

"I promise I'll teach you everything we learn," Kwasi said.

Mesi knew her friend would. Every day, she looked forward to Kwasi coming home. The two could grind millet together, and Kwasi would draw out long division and fractions in the dirt and tell her about the geography of the United States and Europe and South America. It wasn't the same as sitting in a classroom and learning, but Mesi still soaked in every word.

"Someday I'm going to go to the United States," Kwasi would say. "I'm going to live in New York City."

And Mesi believed her. Not many people would leave their small African village, but Kwasi had more drive than twelve people. She'd do it.

The schoolyard was quickly emptying as the students made their way to their classrooms. "You should get inside," Mesi told her friend.

"I will. I've been thinking though, you should talk to Miss Ama about going to school. She is wiser than the teachers. She might have some ideas."

"I never see her anymore." Miss Ama was the wisest woman in the village—probably because she'd lived so long. Kojo, Mesi's brother, had told her Miss Ama was 110 years old. She really didn't believe Miss Ama was that old, but sometimes when she saw the old woman shuffle around her garden, she wondered if it was true.

"Just an idea," Kwasi said, before running off toward the school building. "I'll see you this afternoon," she called. Mesi waved after her.

Mesi picked up her jug and her cornhusk doll, Toolie, who was propped up against it.

"Toolie," she said, clutching the doll.

"I know Kwasi means well, but it doesn't matter how wise Miss Ama is; what I need is money to go to school." For a minute it looked like Toolie's drawn-on eyes actually understood.

Mesi absent-mindedly stroked Toolie's dress as she hiked the two kilometers to the river. Grandmother had given her scraps of lace from the seamstress shop, which Mesi had used to make the dress. It was no wonder Grandmother had nicknamed her "Lacy Mesi" after Mesi's fondness for the material. Grandmother insisted that's why Mesi's name rhymed with the fabric.

"She'd be a fine seamstress," Grandmother had told her father. And Mesi did like to design dresses for her doll. At first she hadn't. She'd wanted her grandmother to make Toolie a dress for her. But Grandmother insisted she would only help Mesi do it herself. Now Mesi was always working on some project or another. Perhaps since she couldn't be a teacher, a seamstress was a good option. Grandmother seemed to enjoy it, and as a bonus, she often had scraps of material for Mesi.

Mesi used an old blanket to tie Toolie to her back, just as the women in the village carried their babies. With both hands free, she leaned down to fill the large jug with water from the slow-moving stream. Even the river showed signs of the drought. The village people said that farther upstream the water levels had gone down dramatically.

A few years ago—when the rainy season had been especially plentiful—she'd come to gather water with her mother, and as she leaned over to fill her jug, a crocodile's eyes had risen out of the water only a few meters away. Mesi's mother had quickly grabbed her and pulled her to the river's edge until the animal was safely downstream. Mesi still got nervous every time she waded into this section of the river, but she knew as low as the water was a crocodile would never make it this far down the river. *I guess that's one good thing about the dry season.* Uncle Yorkoo told everyone that a crocodile is a sign that there is gold in the water, and several of the village men panned that same section. But nothing came of it.

Mesi balanced the filled jug expertly on the top of her head before starting the dusty walk home. It was another warm day, and despite the hard calluses on her bare feet, she could feel the heat from the sand. She knew to hold her head high and straight to keep the jug from falling, but out of the corner of her eye she could see a smattering of acacia trees wavering in a slight breeze.

"Hopefully rain will come soon," she murmured to Toolie, snug against her back. The savannah stretched out around her looking more like a desert. Usually the rainy season would have been here weeks ago, providing months of relief. But this year the dry season dragged on and on. And the cocoa trees weren't growing as many pods as the farmers had hoped. With only a few evening showers here and there, the dry land would need more water if the crops were to produce.

Father didn't typically express his concerns, but she could see the worry in his eyes as day after day he gazed into another cloudless sky. He'd even mentioned his worry to Mother late last night. Only a thin blanket separated the two small rooms in their mud-brick home. She knew Father thought the children were asleep when he said he didn't know if they'd be able to afford another bag of millet and asked Mother to water it down some when she served it to help it last longer.

"Mesi, what took you so long? It's nearly time to start lunch!" Mother called from in front of the house, where she was airing out the dust from the blankets. Baby Jamilah, wrapped onto Mother's back, slept soundly.

Mesi carefully removed the jug from her head and set it on the ground. "I walked by the school," she admitted.

Mother shook her head and folded the blanket.

"I just wanted to see it," Mesi said.

Mother gently put her hand on Mesi's cheek. "I know you want to go to school, but right now we need to focus on getting enough to eat. School may still come, but not this year."

Mesi nodded. But she knew the

harvest would be slim this year, so that meant no school for next year, either.

"Now, Father and Kojo will be coming in from the field soon. If we don't have lunch ready for them, they may eat your jug." Mother smiled, and Mesi noticed the slight creases around her eyes.

"What can I do to help?" asked Mesi.

"Run over to your aunt's house and pick some okra from out back. We can add it to the millet." She handed Mesi a basket. Much of the village consisted of her aunts, uncles, cousins, and grandparents. And the family shared everything they had. So just as Mesi would go to relatives' homes to get okra or yams, the aunts would come to her family's homestead to pick tomatoes.

Mesi felt badly she'd made Mother wait, so she determined to hurry in order to make up for lost time. Which is probably why she didn't notice Miss Ama slowly crossing the path in front of her and ran headlong into the old woman.

"Miss Ama!" Mesi reached out and steadied the frail woman to keep her from toppling over. "I'm so sorry. Please forgive my clumsiness." Mesi felt terribly embarrassed. She cast her eyes down and bowed slightly to the woman to express her apology. Honoring elders was one of the highest values her village carried, and one most certainly didn't treat them with anything less than the highest respect. And here she was running over Miss Ama—the eldest of the wise ones.

Miss Ama's lined face broke into a smile. "You must be in quite a hurry."

"I need to get okra for lunch."

"Then hurry on. You mustn't make your family wait for their lunch."

Mesi made one more apologetic bow. "May I help you home?"

Miss Ama shook her head. "Oh, no, dear. I'm in no hurry. I have all the time in the world."

Mesi gathered her basket which had flown out of her hands. She remembered what Kwasi had said earlier about asking Miss Ama about school. It had seemed out of the question at the time. After all, a ten-year-old simply didn't knock on the hut of the village sage uninvited and ask a question. That would be terribly disrespectful. But perhaps this was her chance. She hesitated.

"Are you all right?" Miss Ama asked, watching her. That was all the invitation Mesi needed. She summoned her courage.

"Miss Ama, my family cannot afford to send me to school, but I so want to go. Do you know of any way that I could attend?"

The words came out in such a nervous rush, Mesi wasn't even sure that Miss Ama could understand them. There was an awkward pause, and Mesi second-guessed even asking. Miss Ama was watching her, almost looking through her, Mesi thought.

"Have you asked God?" Miss Ama asked.

Mesi almost laughed. As though God wandered around the jungles of Africa handing out books and uniforms so young girls could go to school. God most certainly had more important things to do. And he seemed too busy to even make rain. She didn't express any of this to Miss Ama, however.

"No, Miss Ama. That never occurred to me."

"I have no answer to your problem, but if you ask God, he may have an answer."

"Thank you, Miss Ama." *Well, that was a waste of time,* Mesi thought. "I should be going to get the okra now."

"He thinks of you more than you may believe," Miss Ama said, still watching her.

Mesi nodded and excused herself again. But as she collected okra from Aunt Efia's garden, she couldn't help but think of Miss Ama's response. *She acted like God was some personal friend,* Mesi recalled. It didn't make sense. She knew of God. Certainly everyone in her village talked about God, but they also talked about the spirits of ancestors and powers of nature. Who knew who was really in control? And even if God really did have control over things, why would he care about a young girl in the middle of nowhere? But Miss Ama had suggested it—and she was certainly very wise.

Mesi remembered when Mother was struggling while giving birth. She'd previously had two stillborn children, and another looked imminent. But this time Mother was losing so much fluid. Even though Mesi had been young, she knew just by watching Father wring his hands and pace around the fire that Mother was close to death. The village women gathered, chanted, and sang. And then Miss Ama came. She went in with Mother, and an hour later a cry was heard. The baby—Jamilah—survived, and so did Mother. Father called it a miracle. Miss Ama was known to do amazing things.

Mesi filled her basket with the okra. Miss Ama was rarely wrong. *I suppose there's no harm in asking God about school,* Mesi thought. She paused in her picking and bowed her head as she'd heard she was supposed to do.

"God," she said, "I would very much like to go to school. If you could find a way to make that possible, I'd . . . well, I would like that very much."

Mesi looked around. Did she expect God to come out of the cluster of trees behind her aunt's house and give her an answer? *It was a silly thing to do anyway. And now I'm wasting time.* After saying good-bye to her aunt, she hurried home. Mother was already stoking the fire under the iron pot. She poured the millet into the boiling water and stirred it while Mesi chopped the okra and added it to the cooking grain. They ate this meal—*bisap*—every day, although the vegetables they added varied.

Father and Kojo arrived for lunch with Kojo riding on the back of Father's rusty bike. The front wheel wobbled where it had bent. They were both covered with dust and exuded weariness. It was a hot day to work. Kojo took a long drink of water, then joked that maybe Lula, their cow, was eating all the cocoa.

"Perhaps she'll start producing chocolate milk," he said. "Then we'll know the truth."

Mesi giggled while she bounced Jamilah on her lap. She deeply admired her brother. Even when things were difficult, he could get the family to laugh. He had an infectious spark in him that made people happy just being around him. Even Father had to grin at his joke.

Mesi didn't notice the man approaching her family until he stood beside them. A faint bristle of whiskers grew on his dark chin. He looked vaguely familiar to Mesi, but she couldn't place him. The man took off his hat and nodded toward her father.

"Yoofi," said the man bowing his head toward Father.

Father stood up and warmly grasped the man's hand. "*Akwaba,*" Father said, greeting him in the traditional language. "It is good to see you, Abeeku. It has been far too long. Please, join us."

Mother had a full plate of food in front of the man within seconds. Mesi noticed it should have been Mother's plate. She would not be eating lunch today, but they all knew one attended to guests first.

"I have some business to discuss with you," the man said.

Mother nodded to Kojo and Mesi, who quickly excused themselves. Jamilah cooed at Mesi and grasped her tiny fingers into Mesi's short, coarse hair. Mesi slung Jamilah onto her hip.

"Run down to the grove, Mesi, and pick some bananas for you and Jamilah," Mother said.

The bananas were almost gone for the season, but Mesi knew she'd be able to find a few stragglers.

"And bring one down to me," said Kojo. He plopped on his hat and sauntered back to the field.

With Jamilah snuggled against her back, Mesi headed to the banana grove. It was a long walk. She waved to some neighbors as she made her way through the trees. Other families gathered around their lunches or were busy cleaning their dishes. She noticed Miss Ama in her house, staring out the window at something. A bird perhaps? She knew Miss Ama's eyes weren't very good, so she doubted the elderly woman could see her. But Miss Ama lifted a hand in greeting as Mesi passed by the bottom of Miss Ama's hill. Mesi lifted her hand and nodded in return. She was glad

Miss Ama wasn't close enough to ask her about her question for God. But it did remind Mesi about her earlier prayer.

Miss Ama knew how to help her mother deliver Jamilah. She could sense the weather before anyone else. She always knew how to handle tribal feuds. And, Mesi now remembered, she'd told Uncle Yorkoo that crocodiles have nothing to do with locating gold. Maybe . . . just maybe . . . she was right about this, too.

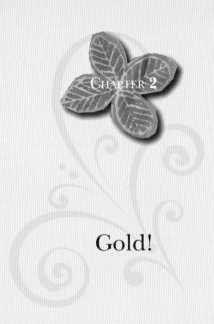

Gold!

Mesi hurried back home with an armload of bananas. Jamilah's sputtering noises reminded Mesi that her little sister must be getting hungry. She was surprised to see Mother hopping around clapping her hands, a big grin plastered across her face. Mesi hadn't seen her mother so happy since Father had come home with a new iron kettle he'd made a trade for at the market.

"What are you so happy about, Mother?" Mesi asked, as she unwound Jamilah from her back.

Mother did three more excited claps and swung Jamilah up in her arms. "That man who came during lunch—Abeeku —asked your father to go on a gold-mining trip with him!"

Gold? Really?

Mesi's mouth dropped open, and mother laughed in response.

"It's true. There's a river up north that Abeeku insists sparkles with gold but hasn't been discovered by the Ewu tribe yet. He's forming a group of men to leave tomorrow." Mother shook her head and sat down on a stump. "Think, Mesi.

Think of what this could mean. With the crops this year. . . ."

Mother didn't need to finish her sentence. Mesi understood. Things had been looking so bleak. The cocoa farm would barely produce anything this year. But if Father came home with baskets of gold, the family would be set—her uncles, aunts, grandparents, and cousins. Mesi grinned. Surely she'd be able to go to school. Surely.

Father emerged from his room, tossing some clothes into a burlap bag. "We'll need some meals for the trip," he said to Mother.

"And some water," Mother noted. She was already sticking some of the bananas Mesi had collected into a bag.

Mesi watched her father. There was something different about him. His eyes seemed brighter. A smile curled on his lips. She decided that must be what hope looks like. The look of believing that things were finally turning around.

"When are you leaving, Father?" she asked.

"Early tomorrow morning," he said.

Mesi clasped her hands in excitement. Then she remembered her prayer. *God did hear,* she thought with disbelief. *Look at what he's done . . . and so quickly!* She'd have to tell Miss Ama when she saw her again. It really worked! She was hopping up and down now, mirroring her mother's excitement.

"Mother, may I go visit Kwasi?" she asked. She knew Kwasi would just be arriving home from school, and this all seemed very urgent to share with her best friend.

"I suppose so, but only for a few minutes." Mother looked very seriously at Mesi. "With your father gone, Kojo will be taking care of the farm. We'll need your help more than ever. You'll need to help him with the field."

Mesi nodded. The thought didn't daunt her. It would be fun to work with Kojo.

Kwasi was stirring up some mud when Mesi arrived.

"We're patching some holes in the roof," Kwasi said, nodding at the thatched covering of their kitchen. Kwasi's homestead was set up differently from Mesi's. One small hut housed Kwasi's father, then next to it was a hut for Kwasi's mother and Kwasi. In two other huts lived Kwasi's father's other wives and their children. The circle was completed by the simple kitchen. Mesi thought it would be neat to have a covered hut to build the fire in when making meals, since her family always cooked outdoors. But she did not envy that Kwasi's father had three wives. Even though it was common for men to marry multiple women, she liked it that her father had only wed her mother.

"Why don't you girls go get some firewood together?" Kwasi's mother suggested.

The story bubbled out of Mesi as the two girls scoured the wooded areas for fallen branches. She told her about running into Miss Ama, her prayer to God, the man who came at lunch, and her father leaving tomorrow to find gold. She took a deep breath as she finished the day's saga. "Can you believe it?" she asked Kwasi.

Kwasi grinned. "I'm so glad you talked to Miss Ama. I wouldn't have expected God to care so much either. But it worked. You did it!"

Mesi loved her friend. She was actually giving Mesi credit for bringing wealth and fortune to her family. "Well, God did it, I suppose."

"Maybe I should start praying for things," Kwasi said. "Like my geography test tomorrow."

"Pretty soon I'll be able to go back to school," Mesi said.

"I know," Kwasi said. "That's the best part of this whole thing."

They carried armloads of tree branches back to Kwasi's mud-brick home.

"Are you excited about your *durbar*?" Mesi asked. Kwasi was having her coming-of-age festival next week. It was one of the most significant times in a girl's life. She was leaving childhood and becoming a woman. The whole village held a huge celebration with food, music, and dancing—all for Kwasi.

Kwasi nodded, causing the sticks to poke into her chin. "Very much. Mother is almost done with my dress."

"I can't wait to see it."

Mesi had mixed feelings about Kwasi's durbar. On one side, it was exciting to have such a big party in honor of her friend, and it was going to be so fun to give Kwasi her gift. For weeks Mesi had been making a shawl out of bits of different laces she'd been saving. She only had to sew on a bit of trim, and the shawl would be done. But, at the same time, Mesi felt sad that her friend would be one more step removed from her. Kwasi would dance in front of all her relatives and friends and get gifts that she would bring into her marriage someday. She'd be toasted and carried up on a chair while the women of the village danced around her. Mesi sighed. Kwasi was going to be a woman soon, and Mesi would still be a girl for two more years.

The girls dumped their wood in a pile by the firepit.

"Will you still play with me?" she asked Kwasi.

Kwasi grabbed Mesi's hand and squeezed it. "I don't know if we can play anymore, but we'll still talk all the time. About everything," she promised.

Mesi nodded. She knew Kwasi would have to be more grown up after her celebration. Mesi thought of Toolie, whom she'd left leaning against a bench at home. Would she have to give up her doll when she became a woman?

Father waved at Mesi from the mammy wagon as it pulled onto the road, leaving a cloud of dust. The bus with open sides was loaded up with about sixty people and a few animals. Most people were heading to a nearby city to sell things at the market. The wagon rocked back and forth as it picked up speed, and Mesi wondered if it would fall apart before it reached the city.

She waved until the truck disappeared beyond the horizon.

Father would probably need to take three or four different wagons to get close to the river spot where they'd mine gold. And then another day's journey on foot, but it would be worth it. When he came home with a load of gold—it would be more than worth it!

The family had woken up early, when the sun was barely peeking over the tops of the acacia trees. Already, the day was warming up. Kojo was giving Mesi instructions for the day at the farm.

"You'll need to weed the whole first half of the grove. I'll show you exactly which ones to pull."

Mesi nodded. Of course, she knew which ones to pull. She'd spent plenty of time in the cocoa field with Kojo. But Kojo was taking his job as man of the house very seriously. And Mesi knew that Kojo wanted to take the best care of the field while Father was gone. And they both knew Father expected nothing less.

The next week went by in a blur. Mesi didn't know when she'd worked so hard. From daybreak to afternoon she'd sweat in the hot sun with Kojo, working in the cocoa field. The large pods hanging from the trees were finally turning yellow, which meant harvesting was near. Already they could pull some down, crack them open, and let the seeds dry. The pods were smaller this year because of the lack of rain, and they would have to make the most out of what they had.

Mesi joked with Kojo that he was more of a slave driver than their father, and Kojo seemed to take it as a compliment. The two would arrive home for their meal with a thick coating of dust stuck to their layers of perspiration.

After a quick meal, Kojo would return to the field and Mesi would start her chores. She had to get water, help with Jamilah, and collect wood. All the things she usually had all day to do, she now had to do in a few hours. She couldn't even think of taking time to walk past the school, and she hadn't seen Kwasi in days.

In the evenings by the flickering light of the fire, she worked on Kwasi's shawl. It seemed more beautiful every time she picked it up. Eventually she dropped into an exhausted sleep, still clutching the material, and Kojo woke her up at dawn the next morning for another full day.

But Friday night was different. When she went down to get water that afternoon, she jumped into the river herself and scrubbed off the week's layers of dirt. She loved the feel of the water on her skin, especially now that the mud no longer caked onto it. She washed the sand out of her hair and even cleaned inside her ears. Then she unpacked her clean dress from the burlap sack she'd brought along. The blue floral dress and vibrant kerchief were reserved for special occasions. She pulled it over her head while the sun stole away the last drops that clung to her legs and hair. It was Kwasi's big party tonight, and she was going to look her best for it.

Men adorned with bright colors beat on drums made of gourds covered with animal skin. They pounded out rhythms while the women danced. A few other men strummed on guitars. The music made the whole earth move—even the trees overhead seemed to pulsate slightly to the rhythm.

Occasionally the men would start a traditional song, and the rest of the people would gather in a circle to dance. As the drumbeat quickened, Mesi's heartbeat did too. She watched as the drumbeat provided the rhythm for dance. Mesi tried to isolate each body movement: her shoulder, then her chest, then her pelvis, an arm, then a leg. Nothing about traditional African dance was stiff. Mesi admired her mother who could dance to the complicated rhythms with different parts of her body moving to the varying beats. Mesi hoped someday she'd be able to dance like that. Mother looked beautiful, dressed in the traditional three-piece dress made of the boldly patterned *Kenti* fabric. Her mother circled up with two of her aunts to perform a dance. Every dance told a story—this particular one was about a man who was out hunting when a hyena chased him. Mesi's family said it was about what happened to Uncle Kwabena two years ago.

Mesi stuffed more fufu in her mouth. The ground yams were so sweet—so good. It had taken a long time for Mesi to grind them into a paste earlier that day, but licking her fingers, she decided it was all worth it. She popped a red-red into her mouth as the plate was passed around. The fried plantain tasted heavenly. Mesi hadn't felt this full in a long time.

The music grew louder, and Mesi noticed Kwasi spinning in front of the musicians. Mesi admired her friend, dancing in a long white dress, her black hair styled in elaborate braids and decorated with a gold-colored headdress. Large hoop earrings hung from her ears, swinging to the rhythm of the music. Mesi knew Kwasi's mother had given her the earrings especially for tonight. Kwasi said they were the same pair her mother had worn at her durbar, and later on her wedding day.

Kwasi was so lithe and graceful, her arms swaying above her head. The sun seemed to set behind her more slowly than usual, as though the light itself didn't want to miss out on the party. Kwasi's aunts, uncles, cousins, grandparents, and people from all across the village and nearly all the surrounding ones moved with her, although none were quite so beautiful. The crowd formed a circle as a new song started. To the beat of the drums, they'd dance, leaning down then standing up, arms held high, while their feet continued dancing. Up and down . . . women in brightly colored head shawls, men with strong limbs and children on their shoulders . . . there was so much to watch. Kwasi sashayed passed Mesi and grabbed her hand. The two girls spun around in circles over and over again. Laughing, they both fell exhausted to the grass. A huge fire was being built up, the adults were laughing, and Mesi noticed that now thousands of stars watched them overhead.

"Just think . . . your father is looking at those same stars tonight, Mesi," Kwasi said, breathless from laughing.

"But not having nearly as much fun," said Mesi. It felt good to rest on her back after all the dancing.

"The stars look like gold to me," decided Kwasi. "I think that means that your father must have found gold. Lots of it."

"They do look gold. They look like dancing specks of

gold," agreed Mesi. "Oh! I have something for you," she said, pulling Kwasi to her feet. "It's by the field."

"I can't leave," said Kwasi.

"Only for a minute. Please." The two girls ran off to the cocoa field where Mesi had tucked her precious gift under a makeshift bench—a slab of wood balanced precariously on two stones. The field was just behind Kwasi's homestead, and they could still hear the talking and singing as they huddled on the bench.

Mesi pulled out the shawl, proud of how the silver beads shimmered in the moonlight. She was proud of how even in the dark, the intricacy of the design was evident. She gently let the material pour into Kwasi's hands. "Here. It's a shawl for a true woman—like you."

Kwasi's eyes became the size of saucers. "Mesi . . . this is. . . ."

Mesi could hear her friend crying.

"This is so beautiful. Thank you. I love it." She wrapped her arms around Mesi, burying her face into Mesi's shoulder. "You are such a dear chalay; you're a sister."

The girls heard Kwasi's mother calling her.

"You need to get back," Mesi said.

Kwasi nodded. "Yes, but I'm almost nervous for my mother to see this. My aunts gave me such beautiful shawls, but none as beautiful as this. I don't want them to see it. They'd feel bad."

Mesi understood. It would be disrespectful for a child such as herself to show up the aunts who traditionally gave the finest gifts. She didn't want to do anything to dishonor Kwasi's family.

"We'll put it back in the bag, and I'll give it back to you after your time in seclusion." It was tradition for the young woman to be put in isolation for eight days after her durbar.

Kwasi shook her head vigorously. "No. I don't want to leave it here."

"It will be fine. We'll keep it in the bag. And I'll get it and take care of it until I see you next."

Kwasi reluctantly handed back the shawl. "Okay. Only eight days." She seemed to be convincing herself of the shawl's safety.

"Kwasi! Come quickly!" Kwasi's mother called.

"Come with me!" Kwasi said.

Mesi set the bag gently under the bench and went with her friend back to the party.

They danced more and sang all the traditional songs. And Kwasi showed off the shawls she'd received from her aunts, each of them jibing the other by insisting hers was the loveliest, the most special. But Mesi knew the truth. Then Kwasi performed her own dance. Her mother and grandmother had been the only ones to see it before, as they had coached her practices for months. The rest of the crowd watched breathlessly as Kwasi moved about, encircling the fire, flipping and twirling her body and the cloth flags attached to her arms and legs, telling the story of a migrating bird. She was beautiful.

The party went very late. Finally, Mother tugged at Mesi's arm. "We need to go. You have to work in the field tomorrow." Mesi nodded. Even with all the excitement, she was beginning to feel the heaviness of her eyelids. Jamilah was fast asleep on Mother's back, and Kojo had already gone home, so the two walked in silence back to the homestead.

Mesi smiled, tired but content. She wondered how Father was doing. He was probably sitting around the fire drinking coffee, laughing with his friends. She imagined them sifting through the bags of gold, watching it fall through their fingers. Perhaps they were talking about their families back home and sharing what they were going to do with their new-found wealth.

Thank you, God, Mesi prayed.

Just then, a drop of water plopped on the top of her head. Mesi looked up. Another one hit her shoulder, then her nose. She looked at her mother, who was also staring up at the sky. Mesi watched Mother lift her palms, catching the drops—now coming more quickly—in her hands. Mother looked down at Mesi, her white smile clear even in the dark of night. They hoped this meant the drought was over. The rainy season had finally arrived!

Could life get any better?

In her dream that night, Mesi danced. Gold was pouring from the sky and into the windows—like a flood of raindrops. She was spinning and twirling with the lacy shawl she'd made for Kwasi. The material floated effortlessly amidst the sparkling coins. She felt rocked back and forth.

"Mesi! Mesi!" Her mother was shaking

her awake, shouting over the sound of the rain pounding on the tin roof.

Mesi forced herself out of her dream. There was an urgency in her mother's voice. Something . . . something was going on.

Before she could form the words to ask, Mother explained. "The cocoa field was struck by lightning. It's on fire. You need to go help Kojo." Mesi could see the terror in her mother's eyes and knew it was reflected in her own. *The cocoa field.* That was all they had.

CHAPTER 3

Cocoa Field

Mesi wondered if she was still dreaming except she could feel the rain pressing the clothes against her skin. She could smell the smoldering of the cocoa plants—like how burnt chocolate must smell. She could feel the heat of the fire, even though she was still a ways from it.

And the look on Kojo's face—she could never dream a face like that. She'd never seen anything like it: horrified, scared, and disbelieving. A dozen men from the village were there with him, frantically pouring buckets of water onto the growing fire. More men were running down the hill.

"Go! Help your brother! Now!" Mother had shouted. And Mesi had been out the door— somehow pulling on clothes that she now had no memory of putting on. Her side ached from running as fast as she could down to the field. But she kept going. She had to. *The cocoa field . . . the cocoa field. . . .* The mantra ran through her head over and over. It was what she could hear her mother wailing as she ran out of the house—even over the thunder and pouring rain.

Despite the rain, the fire seemed intent on overtaking

the field. The men from the village carried logs on bare shoulders, trying to cut off the fire's path. Mesi found herself in a bucket brigade that soon proved futile, yet they kept passing the buckets—hoping the next one would make a dent in the raging inferno.

Mesi knew all the men of the village were here. Nothing happened to anyone that everyone else wasn't involved in. Through death, sickness, tragedy, the building of a new home, the start of a marriage—they were all family. They all looked out for one another. Countless times Father had given money to help neighbors, Kojo had fixed broken wagons, Mother had nursed ailing infants. Now it was their turn to receive from the community.

Kojo grabbed her, nearly whacking her with the log he held on his shoulder. "Go get Lulu. The fire's moving in that direction!" Mesi ran toward the shanty where the cow was tied inside.

A cattle mansion. That's what Father had said when they'd built the shack.

"This cow's going to have the nicest place to live this side of the river." Lulu had given them milk for years. She was nearly as much a part of their livelihood as the cocoa field.

Mesi could tell the fire was heading west toward the wooden lean-to and north toward the woods. How could this have happened so quickly? The joy and thrill she'd felt the night before now seemed as fallen as the puddles of rain she was sloshing through. It all seemed so far away . . . the dancing, the singing, the excitement of giving Kwasi her shawl.

The shawl!

Mesi remembered that she'd left it tucked under the bench. The bench on the other side of the field. Without a second thought, she changed direction and raced toward it. She could see the brown burlap sack. The nearing flames seemed to be taunting her, as they were ready to lick it up, ready to consume the beautiful shawl. She stumbled across the bench, knocked over the stones, and grabbed the sack. Then she ran away from the fire as fast as she could. But she could still hear Kojo.

"Mesi! The cow!"

His shout was more like a scream. She rushed back through the woods, the heat of the fire and the smoke filling her eyes. She wasn't even sure she was heading in the right direction. She should have gotten Lulu first. But she hadn't even thought. She knew she'd had to rescue the shawl. *Somehow I need to make it back. I need to get Lulu.* But the smoke was getting thicker, weighing down on her like a quilt. Coughing and wheezing, she finally made it to a place where she could breathe, out of the way of the billowing gray haze. A crack of dawn's light unsuccessfully tried to make its rays penetrate the smoke cloud.

She turned to see that she'd run up the hill at the north end of the field. She hadn't even realized she'd been going uphill. She could now see an overhead view of the fire. Lines of logs and ditches blocked it from getting to the north side of the field, but the flames were still moving west. The cow barn was only a shadow in the smoke. She held her breath. Kojo was beating down the west wall of the barn, pulling at what Mesi knew had to be Lulu. It seemed like a cruel race. The flames versus Kojo. The hay thatching that made up the shanty's roof burst into flames as though a bomb had gone off, and the structure collapsed.

"No!" Mesi started to scream. But nothing came out. She was running down the hill, and then slipping, sliding with her face in the mud. She got up to see the cow walking out of the cloud of smoke. And then two men carrying Kojo, a limp, unmoving Kojo.

Kojo was still unconscious as Uncle Yorkoo carried him back to the homestead. The last few hours had gone by in a blur, but now every step seemed exceedingly slow. No one knew how badly Kojo was injured. He'd occasionally drift back into consciousness, so Mesi continued to hold onto his hand to give him some assurance that she was there.

Uncle Yorkoo was telling the other village men, "I'm not sure how he got out of there. I ran into that inferno, and there he was lying on the edge. That beam came down on his leg pretty hard though."

Mesi noticed that Kojo's pants were melted to parts of his leg. Her tears dripped down her nose and fell into the puddles on the ground, making tiny muddy splashes.

The rain had stopped, and the sun was beginning to rise, sending rays of tangerine-colored light across the horizon.

Birds were singing songs, as though they were happy there would be some insects to snack on today. It was a beautiful morning, which seemed nonsensical. How could a day start so lovely when the night before had been so painful and hard? How could the world have such beauty, when all she felt was misery?

Kojo moaned, and Mesi looked at him. His eyes slowly focused, and he groaned with every one of Uncle Yorkoo's jerking steps.

"I'm so sorry," Mesi whispered to him. "It's my fault. I was supposed to get the cow. I'm so sorry."

Kojo squeezed her hand—hard. "It wasn't your job. It was mine. It was my fault." He fell silent for so long that Mesi thought he'd slipped back into unconsciousness. But then he muttered. "Or it was God's fault."

Mesi felt her heart flip. Only hours ago, she'd thought God had given her everything she could want. Could he hurt them, too? Was he angry at Mesi? Was this his punishment? Maybe it was the payment for Father getting gold. Maybe there was a sacrifice that had to be made. She'd never thought of that. She'd never thought of the price. After all, what had she done to earn God's favor?

Mesi winced as Kojo winced.

"This will only be another minute," Mother said as she pressed the gauze on Kojo's leg. Underneath the stark whiteness of the bandage, the blackened blisters trailed up Kojo's leg.

For the hundredth time, Mesi wished she could take her brother's place. Although she was relieved that he'd made it out of the fire alive, the damage had been done. He had severe burns down his right leg and a broken foot. Mother had asked Uncle Yorkoo to place Kojo on her and Father's bed, instead of on the straw mat the children shared. Now shreds of blackened skin and dried blood tainted the once-clean sheets. Mother was trying her best to care for him, as were the other women in the village. It seemed like every twenty minutes someone was coming by with a salve or some cornmeal or a word of encouragement.

As Mother cleaned and dressed the wounds, Mesi continued to hold Kojo's hand, searching for something—anything— that would take his mind off the pain.

"Think of all the gold Father will bring back," she said. "We'll be able to buy a whole new field. And ten cows."

"And he probably won't trust me with any of them after what happened," Kojo replied through gritted teeth. Mesi knew he was trying not to yelp from the pain.

"Mesi, let your brother rest," Mother said. In other words, *Be quiet. Don't say anything to upset him.*

Mesi wanted to say that she only meant to cheer him up. She didn't want to make him feel guilty. If anyone should feel guilty, it should be Mesi. She was the one who didn't listen. She was the one who ran in the other direction to save a stupid shawl. But she didn't say any of this.

"We'll need more water, Mesi," Mother said, wringing out a rag she'd used to clean Kojo's wounds.

Mesi could see the concern on Mother's face. She knew Mother didn't feel like she was doing enough for Kojo. The injuries were too severe. And a broken foot was difficult to set. She knew her mother felt the weight of the world on her—three children to take care of by herself, a severely burned son, and never far from any of their minds, the still-smoldering cocoa field.

Grabbing her bucket and strapping Jamilah to her back, Mesi hurried out the door. There wasn't much she could do for her brother, but she'd hurry and do what she could.

"Mesi? How's your brother?" Miss Ama's wavering voice filtered down the hillside to where Mesi walked, returning with the water.

"Not very good, Miss Ama," Mesi said. "He's very hurt."

Miss Ama nodded. "I will come over later to see how I can help. In the meantime, I will pray."

Pray. Mesi felt her shoulders tighten at the thought.

"Thank you, Miss Ama," said Mesi, watching her bare toes make circles in the dirt. "But please don't."

"Why, child?"

"I'm afraid it will make things worse. See . . . I think maybe this all happened because I prayed to go to school, and so God sent Father to get gold, but now we have to pay the price." She took a deep breath. "And I don't want to owe God anything else."

Miss Ama lifted a shaking hand and placed it on Mesi's shoulder. "It seems like it should work that way. And with many of the so-called gods in this country—in this whole continent of Africa—we've always been taught

to make sacrifices or perform rituals to have our prayers answered. But that's not the way this God is—the one true God. He doesn't need those things from us."

"Then why did he do this to Kojo?" Mesi tried unsuccessfully to wipe her tears away before they were noticeable. They kept falling. "Why would he do this to us?"

"I suppose that's what makes God who he is. He doesn't have to answer or explain himself. He simply is. And we can't understand his ways."

"Well, I don't like that."

"I don't think he's done with your story yet, Mesi. God is still at work. I know it." Miss Ama steadied herself on Mesi's arm. "God is good." Her aged hand squeezed Mesi's wrist.

Mesi excused herself and headed on her way. She didn't believe Miss Ama. None of this made sense. How could God be good? And she really didn't like the idea of God being "still at work" in her life.

After all, what terrible thing was he going to do next?

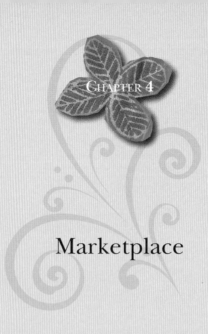

Marketplace

Jamilah was cooing as they walked back to the homestead. Mesi was just rounding the path and could see the thatched roof of their mud home. *Was that. . . . It was! Father was home!* She wanted to sprint the rest of the way, but that was easier said than done with a jug of water on her head and a baby on her back. She couldn't make out anything he'd brought home, but she imagined he and Mother were talking about what they would do with all the gold he'd brought. Or maybe he'd already exchanged it for money in town. Of course that would make the most sense. And since he was in town, he probably picked up treats for them. He knew how Mesi loved chocolate candy, or maybe he'd gotten her a real doll to play with Toolie. Not that she would ever give up her cornhusk friend, but how fun it would be to have a sister for her! One with moveable legs and bright eyes. Father would get Mother a new cast-iron pot, Kojo a bicycle of his own so he wouldn't have to borrow Father's, and Jamilah a pair of little shoes.

As she got closer, she could see the seriousness written across Father's face. Of course he was probably sad that Kojo got hurt, but surely all the money he got from the gold would cheer them all up. Right?

"Father! Welcome home!" she called.

"Mesi. Take that water in to your brother. He needs a drink."

That was it. No "I have something for you" or "Get ready to go to school next year." Not even a smile.

Kojo was sleeping when Mesi went inside the room. She filled up his tin cup with water. Her parents spoke outside, not noticing that Mesi had left the door ajar.

"We searched fourteen hours a day, even into the night. Nothing," Father said.

"But Abeeku was so certain. He said the river glowed of gold," Mother said.

"Well, at least at the part we were at, there was nothing glowing. Then the Ewus approached our site late one night. They said they were claiming the river and we were trespassing. If we weren't out of there by morning, our lives would be taken."

"I'm glad you made it out safely."

"Yes, but with nothing. An entire two weeks there and nothing to show for it. I would have been better off being here. At least then I could have protected my field." Father paused. "Protected my son."

Mesi absent mindedly placed a wet cloth on Kojo's forehead. Feelings of guilt weighed on the entire family. She felt it. Kojo felt it. And, now, even her father.

"You had no idea," Mother said. "You were trying to do what was best for all of us."

"I thought it was my chance. Finally, the gods were smiling down on me. But I guess that wasn't the case."

Mesi could hear Mother take the coffee pot off the fire and pour a cup for Father. "What do you think we should do for Kojo? He needs more help than I'm able to give," she said. "I wish I knew how to help him more."

Add Mother to the list of guilt-bearers.

"I don't think we have any other choice. You're going to have to go into the city. To the hospital."

"We can't afford that. And how would we make the trip? Someone will need to watch Jamilah while I'm with Kojo," Mother said. Mesi leaned in closer to the crack of the door to hear as Mother's voice grew quieter. "I don't know if we can."

"You have to. Kojo needs it," Father answered. "Mesi will go along to help."

"What about you?"

"I'll start re-planting the field. I'll try to salvage what's left."

Mesi had always thought her first trip into town would be much more exciting than this. She sat crammed in the mammy wagon, while friends of her mother continued to stuff gifts and merchandise around her. It was typical of neighbors to be like family, but she knew the women of the village had outdone themselves. There were baskets and baskets of things to sell at the market, to earn money for Kojo's medical expenses. People in her village didn't have a lot to give—they were all suffering because of the drought, and no one ever had a lot of surplus. But that didn't keep them from giving. They gave until they couldn't give anymore. It was just who they were.

Grandmother's wrinkled smile stood out from the others.

Most of her teeth were missing, but Mesi still thought she had the most beautiful smile. Grandmother waved a small brown paper bag at her.

"I have a gift for you." She reached up to hand it to Mesi.

"Something else to sell?" Mesi asked. "But you already gave Mother a whole basket of handbags."

"This is for you. It will give you something to do while you wait."

"Thank you, Grandmother." Mesi smiled. She didn't think she deserved a gift. Kojo deserved one for enduring all he had. Father deserved something for working so hard and coming up empty-handed. Mother deserved one for the way in which she cared for everyone. But Mesi didn't believe she deserved anything.

The truck lurched beneath her, throwing her off balance. She waved with the rest of the passengers to the crowd behind them as the vehicle bounced along the dusty road. It should have been fun and exciting to be traveling to the city. She'd wanted to go for as long as she could remember. She and Kwasi had spent long hours talking about what they would do if they ever had the chance to go. *Kwasi.* She missed her friend. She hadn't had a chance to see her because of Kwasi's seclusion. She wanted to tell her she saved her shawl, but even more she wanted her shoulder to cry on right now. She never thought she'd be going to town under these circumstances. How could she enjoy it when she saw her brother's face clench in pain with every jolt of the lumbering truck? It would be a very long ride for him. And she didn't know what to expect when they got there. Mother said she'd be in charge of selling things at the market, but she'd never done anything like that before. And she'd probably have to watch Jamilah throughout the day, as well.

She peeked inside the paper bag Grandmother had handed her. Dozens of pieces of lace and silk lay folded inside. Some of them were tiny scraps, but all together they would make beautiful dresses for her doll. She hugged the cornhusk baby closer to her. *If nothing else, I'll have the best-dressed doll in the country.*

She steeled her face toward the horizon. The road seemed to go on eternally, over hills and through fields. It was hard to believe that only a week ago her father had left on this same truck. It was hard to believe the hope and excitement they'd all felt. How everything had seemed so wonderful. So promising.

And it was even harder to believe she once thought God cared.

Mesi set out the straw purses with colorful embroidery, wood-carved figurines, head kerchiefs, and fresh vegetables. The makeshift booth wasn't very sturdy and shifted under the weight. Soon people started arriving and bartering for her wares. Mesi loved the bustle of the market. It was so different from life back home which was always slow and predictable. Here there were people of all different shapes and sizes, dressed in all different types of clothing. People had different accents and spoke in different languages. Some were tourists looking for a souvenir. Most were townspeople out to buy produce for their daily meals.

She'd been surprised by the vast array of goods that were available.

She'd never seen some of these things. Among the typical huge baskets of grain, wide-brimmed hats, and stacks of colorful clothes were booths that specialized in shiny silver bracelets, tiny cars used as toys, and huge bouquets of colorful flowers. One booth even had chocolate. Despite the fact that her father ran a cocoa field, she'd only tried the delicacy once. Her family didn't see the cocoa all the way through the chocolate process. They collected the pods, scooped out the seeds, dried them, and then Father took them to the city to sell. There, manufacturing plants would finish the process. But once he had returned with a chocolate bar for the family to share. Mesi placed a little bit on her tongue and let it melt there, savoring every morsel.

More than once, Mesi thought about how much Kwasi would have loved to see all this. She tried to memorize every detail so she could tell her friend about it later.

"How much for the purse?" asked a woman. Mesi was finally getting used to this part of her job—bargaining. She'd tell the woman a very high price for the purse, the woman would offer her something very low, and they would go back and forth and agree on a price somewhere in the middle.

Customers gathered all around her booth, picking up the items, asking prices, bartering.

The morning went by quickly in all of its busyness. Mesi was collecting a good amount of money. Mother arrived mid-day with Jamilah on her back.

"I brought you some lunch," she said. She opened a cloth to reveal some bread and fruit.

Up until that point Mesi had been too busy to even think about eating. But seeing the food in front of her reminded her how hungry she was.

"Thank you." Mesi reached for a piece of bread. "How's Kojo?"

Mother nodded. "Good, all things considered. We saw the doctor this morning. He reset Kojo's foot so it will heal properly and was able to treat the burns. He also gave your brother some pain medication so he could sleep."

Mesi was relieved that Kojo was finally out of pain. "Where is he now?"

"Resting in the hospital. We have another appointment this afternoon." Mother removed Jamilah from her back and swaddled her tightly in the blanket. Jamilah stirred slightly in her sleep. "I'd like you to watch Jamilah for the next few hours."

"That should be easy enough." Already Mesi could tell the crowds were thinning out as the sun rose higher in the sky. The heat would keep most people away in the afternoon. "Is Kojo going to be all right?"

"I think so," Mother said. "I'm glad we came. The doctor was so helpful. Although it took us nearly five hours to be able to see him."

Mesi remembered people saying that lines outside clinics would often stretch all the way around the building. She imagined her mother and brother must have waited like that. The clinic they'd gone to was charity sponsored, and there was only one doctor to see hundreds of patients.

Mother fiddled with some embroidery on one of the purses. "Kojo will be on crutches for quite some time, though. You'll need to help out with the farm more."

Mesi nodded. She didn't meet her mother's eyes but knew she must be thinking the same thing. *How much farm would be left to help with?* She pictured Father back home and wondered how he was doing. She knew the men in the town would be helping out as much as they could, but there was only so much anyone could do.

Mother glanced through Mesi's cash box. "You did well this morning," she noted.

"It was busy."

Mother tucked Mesi's chin in her palm. "You're a good girl, Mesi."

Mesi appreciated her mother's words, but she didn't feel like she could believe them.

After Mother left, Mesi straightened her table, calling out her wares to the occasional passersby. But her thoughts before lunch had been correct. The hot afternoon was far less busy. And the shabby canopy hanging over the booth barely allowed enough shade for her and Jamilah, much less gave customers any needed relief from the sun.

Some of the neighboring vendors began to pack up for the day.

"Will we see you tomorrow?" asked the portly woman who had set up beside her. She'd been selling figs and sweets.

"I'll be here all week, as long as my wares hold out."

"See you tomorrow then," the woman turned to leave, balancing one basket on her head, and two others on each arm. The pouch with her day's money was slung across her shoulder. Without looking back, she called, "Take a break. There won't be much going on this afternoon. And I saw how hard you worked this morning."

"Thank you," Mesi called after her. "See you tomorrow."

Mesi knew she couldn't break down the booth. Even if she made one more sale today, it would provide a little more much-needed income. Besides, what would she do for the afternoon if she wasn't here? They were staying in a nearby tent town—which was essentially thousands of tents set up for people who'd been displaced because of wars in neighboring regions. Everything was so close together. And Mesi found the whole scene depressing—so many people talking about lost homes and family members. She'd much rather be here, even in the sweltering heat.

Mesi cast a glance at Jamilah, who was still sleeping soundly, and then up and down the empty dirt alleyway. *I might as well do something to keep me busy,* she thought. She pulled out a dress she'd been working on for Toolie with the scraps that Grandmother had given her. She'd started it around the fire in the tent town last night. It helped distract her from her worries. She'd used a gold satin piece for the bodice and layered the skirt with lace and sparkly gold silk. It reminded her of a princess's wedding dress. It looked royal. All she needed to do was hem the skirt.

Mesi must have been completely absorbed in her work, because she didn't notice the woman watching her until the woman cleared her throat.

Mesi jumped in surprise, dropping the dress. "I'm sorry. May I help you? Are you looking for a handbag? A souvenir?"

"I was actually looking at the dress you were working on." The woman was one of the most beautiful Mesi had ever seen. Her dark chocolate skin was smooth and soft, and long earrings dangled down to her shoulders on each side of her oval face. She smiled, nodding at the sleeping baby. "Is it for your sister?"

"It's actually for my doll," Mesi said. She held up the dress to show how little it was.

The woman reached for it, running her fingers along the lace. "I've never seen such an elegant dress for a doll. Did you make this yourself?"

"Yes, ma'am," Mesi said. She couldn't place the woman's accent but, judging from the beautiful clothing she wore, decided she must be pretty well off.

"Do you have some for sale?"

"Oh, no. I'm not a professional seamstress, ma'am." Mesi wondered why anyone would be interested in buying her doll clothes. She was the only girl she knew who interchanged her doll's outfits. And why would an adult, of all people, ask that?

"But your work is exquisite." The woman examined the dress more closely. "This is made better than my own clothes. What is your name?"

Mesi looked the woman up and down, knowing that her compliment couldn't be true. Her clothing was beautiful. She replied sheepishly, "Mesi."

The woman reached into her purse, pulled out a bill from her wallet, and pressed it into Mesi's palm. "Will you sell this one to me?"

"Sell?" Mesi couldn't believe what she was hearing.

"Yes. Is that enough?" Mesi looked down at the bill. It was more than enough. She could make ten dresses for the amount this woman was paying for one!

"Yes . . . yes," Mesi felt her head swim. She didn't even know what to say. "But the dress isn't even done. I'm still finishing up the skirt."

"I'll be back tomorrow then. Can you finish it tonight?"

"Of course. Of course." Mesi tried to hand the bill back, but the woman waved it away.

"No, you keep that. I'll see you tomorrow." She looked at the dress again. Mesi held her breath. Surely this woman would come to her senses and change her mind. Right now, she was probably noticing all the flaws, thinking how silly it was to buy such an ornate dress for a doll. Mesi wondered if perhaps the hot sun was making the woman delusional.

But instead the woman said, "How long would it take you to make another one?"

"I can usually make one in a few hours."

"That's all? You're very talented."

"Thank you, ma'am."

"Do you think you could make another one for me tonight? I'll pay you the same—even a little more since I'm rushing you."

Mesi thought perhaps she was the delusional one. Maybe the sun was causing her to imagine things. She shut her eyes tight and then reopened them.

But the woman still stood there with an expectant look on her face.

"That . . . that should be fine," Mesi stammered.

"Wonderful. I'll be back tomorrow then. By the way, my name is Makeena."

CHAPTER 5

Grace!

"I couldn't believe it, Mother! She really loved the doll dress that much!"

Mother stared at the money in Mesi's outstretched palm after hearing the story of Miss Makeena.

"Amazing. You make beautiful clothes for Toolie, but I certainly never thought it would be profitable."

"Well, selling two dresses won't make us rich, but it's something." Already Mesi was wondering if Miss Makeena would come back. Perhaps she thought of Mesi as a charity case and was looking for a nice way to give her money. Or maybe she would come to her senses overnight and would come back tomorrow to ask for a refund.

"It's wonderful news, Mesi," Mother said. "Why do you look so sad?"

"I just wonder if she was for real . . . if she'll be back."

Mother gave Mesi a hug. "Don't be so worried. I'm doing enough worrying for both of us. And it doesn't do any good anyway."

The fire flickered in front of them, and Mother stirred

the pot of millet with a big spoon. Jamilah played in the dirt a safe distance from the fire. Kojo slept soundly in the tent. Mesi was glad the medication for his pain seemed to be working. He was in a better mood when they returned to the camp.

"I'm going to wake Kojo up and have him eat something. He'll need strength to recover." Mother disappeared inside the tent with a full clay bowl.

Mesi stared up at the sky, noticing the stars for the first time since Kwasi's party—when they'd danced and celebrated along with the people at the party. They looked the same tonight but maybe not as happy. She remembered her and Kwasi's dream of gold as they watched the stars sparkle. Now that seemed so long ago.

♡ ♡ ♡

Mesi impatiently shifted from one foot to the other. For what seemed like the hundredth time, she looked down the corridor of booths to see if Miss Makeena was coming. Mesi was almost certain the woman had changed her mind. She'd only slept a few hours the night before, and they'd been restless ones. She dreamt about the night of the fire and woken up with a tear-stained face.

"Will you give me a discount if I buy two baskets?" the American tourist in front of her asked, her camera swinging across her belly.

Mesi forced herself to stop thinking about Miss Makeena and focused on selling her other things.

After bartering for a few minutes, the woman paid and left. It was still early, but a whole crowd had swarmed around

Mesi now. Perhaps word had spread from the day before about the quality of products she carried. Mesi knew the women in her village worked very hard to make their baskets and handbags flawless with beautiful embroidery.

"Mesi!" a woman called. Mesi recognized the bright smile instantly. She had returned!

"Miss Makeena! You came back!"

"Of course, I did, child!" Miss Makeena laughed. "I want my dresses."

Miss Makeena looked at the second dress carefully, and Mesi held her breath.

"This isn't like the other one," Miss Makeena murmured.

Mesi's heart dropped into her bare feet. "I'm sorry. I didn't know you wanted an identical one! I didn't have the same material. I can remake it."

"No, no." Miss Makeena smiled. "I was only saying that this one is even more beautiful than the other one. I didn't know if you'd be able to make it as nice as the first since you only had an evening to work on it. But I'm astounded that you've surpassed the quality. I'm very, very pleased."

Happy tears sprung to Mesi's eyes. She'd so wanted Miss Makeena to love it.

Miss Makeena pulled out her handbag. "And therefore I insist on paying you more for this one." She handed Mesi twice as much as she had the day before.

"But this is too much!" Mesi blurted out.

"Nonsense," Miss Makeena said. "An excellent craftswoman should always be rewarded for her fine talent."

An excellent craftswoman. The beautiful words rolled around Mesi's brain.

"Is your mother alive?" Miss Makeena asked.

Mesi understood the question. Most girls her age who worked at booths in the market were trying to help support their families because their mothers had died.

Mesi nodded. "Yes. She'll be here in the afternoon. She's at the hospital with my brother."

Miss Makeena nodded. "I'll come back to talk with her this afternoon."

Mother was in a better mood when she came by that afternoon. The doctor said that Kojo was healing well and they would be able to head back home the day after tomorrow. Living in the tent city had taken a toll on all of them. Their small cinder block home was modest, but at least it was theirs. And it felt safe with Father there to protect them.

"I can't wait to put my feet in the river again," Mesi said.

Mother nodded. "And watch the sun set over the trees."

"And not be crowded in with so many people." In the tent city, the tents all pressed up against each other in the crowded space. She could hear the talking, snoring, and crying all night long.

"It will be wonderful to be home again," Mother said.

Mesi had sold nearly all the merchandise the village women had given them, and that added to Mother's happiness. "This, along with what you received from Miss Makeena, will be enough to pay for Kojo's medical bills."

Mesi was glad that she could contribute to her brother's treatment. She still felt guilty about the accident, even though Kojo had told her repeatedly that it wasn't her fault.

"Miss Makeena said she wanted to come by and see you this afternoon," Mesi said.

"I'll be happy to meet her. She's done a great service for our family."

As if on cue, Miss Makeena approached.

"You must be Mesi's mother," she said, extending her hand.

Mother took it. "Hello, Miss Makeena. I'm so happy to meet you." Mother gave a small bow. "You've been so kind to my daughter."

"She has been so kind to me," Miss Makeena said. "I've rarely received such fine clothing as she's made for me. In fact, that's what I wanted to talk to her more about. And you, as well."

"How may we help you?" Mother asked.

"I grew up in this area, but I've since moved to Britain and now own a small shop. I would love to be able to sell Mesi's doll clothes in my store."

Mesi's eyes widened.

"Do you mean the two dresses she already made you?" Mother asked.

"I mean that I would love for Mesi to keep sending me dresses that I can sell. I'm prepared to pay her in advance for ten of them, including the cost to ship them."

"Are you sure?" Mesi asked. She knew it was disrespectful to interrupt her mother's conversation, but she was in such disbelief she had to ask. This didn't seem possible. Ten dresses? Sold in England?

"Of course, I'm sure," Miss Makeena said. "And then I'll probably want ten more each month.

I expect them to sell very well. But we'll start out with that amount and work up. Can you manage to make that many, Mesi?"

"Yes, yes, of course!"

"And feel free to be creative with them. I trust the designer in you. God has clearly given you great talent."

God. Mesi hadn't thought about God since they left the village. Could this have anything to do with God?

♡ ♡ ♡

Mesi ran to greet her father, her legs carrying her as quickly as they could go. He held out his arms and swung her up into a giant bear hug.

"Father, you won't believe what happened!"

It wasn't until Mother caught up with them carrying Jamilah, Kojo wobbled up on his crutches, and the mammy wagon pulled away that the whole story finally poured out.

"Mesi, that is wonderful. I'm so proud of you," Father said.

"I'll be able to help now with money since the field is damaged."

"You are a good daughter. We may need some of that to get by the next few months. But, fortunately, the field isn't as damaged as we first expected. We'll still harvest over half of the cocoa—and because of the rain, it should be a decent crop."

"That's good to hear," Mother said.

"Perhaps it all happened for a reason. The trees that burned were older, and they'd become less productive. We will plant new ones and surround them with cola nuts. The two crops complement each other, and that will tide us over while the cocoa grows back."

"So we're going to grow cola nuts, too?" Mesi asked.

"Yes. Then in five years, the cocoa trees will be producing better than ever. Things will be tight until then, but we'll make do."

"Yes, we'll manage," Mother said, giving Mesi a squeeze. "If we can get through this together, we will only be stronger."

Father turned to Mother. "And Grandmother mentioned to me after you left that the regional chief has started using her seamstress shop for himself and his representatives. She's so busy that she needs extra help. Would you be interested in working part time there?"

Mother nodded. "I would. I'll need some extra help at home though."

The four started back to their home.

Mesi felt the relief wash over her. Things were going to be all right. "I can watch Jamilah while you're working," she offered.

"I think I can take her with me," Mother said slowly. She cast a glance at Father and then turned back to Mesi. "Since you'll be making money now, you should decide what you want to get for yourself."

Mesi had been so concerned about Kojo's health and the rest of her family, she hadn't even considered getting anything for herself. She really didn't need anything, except . . . except one thing.

"Do you think I could go back to school?" she asked.

"I think that would be a wonderful idea," Mother said.

"Yes," Father agreed, a beaming grin on his face. "You should go back to school."

Mesi didn't think her feet touched the ground all the way home.

"Let's meet together to study after dinner," called Kwasi as she veered off the path to her own home.

"Yes," Mesi agreed. "That will give me time to do my chores." She readjusted her backpack, relishing the feeling of all the books inside it. Books on history and geography, math, and grammar. She loved them all.

"I especially need to work on my division tables," Kwasi said. She squeezed Mesi's hand. "I'm so glad I get to go to school with you again."

"Me, too," Mesi said.

She headed up the path, humming a song in her head.

"Well, greetings little Mesi."

The voice seemed to come from the trees, but when Mesi turned she saw Miss Ama leaning against her walking stick and carrying a basket of grain.

"Hello, Miss Ama," she said. "May I help you with your basket?"

Miss Ama handed it to her and hobbled alongside her down the path. "So did your father find gold?"

"No, Father didn't find gold," she said.

"And yet," Miss Ama nodded toward Mesi's backpack, "it appears as though you are back in school."

"Yes," Mesi said, smiling. "It's a long story, but somehow it all worked out."

"Ah," Miss Ama said. "Somehow."

Mesi stared down at the stones scattered along the path. "I don't know if God helped, Miss Ama. Nothing happened like I expected, like I thought it would. Father was supposed to find gold."

"Child, you received what you prayed for. You received your gold."

Mesi was confused. Hadn't Miss Ama heard her?

"Excuse me, Miss Ama?"

"I was thinking of how a few years ago your grandmother told me that you had asked her to make a dress for your doll, and she gave you scrap material from the shop instead."

"That's right," Mesi remembered. She had wanted just a simple dress for her doll, nothing nearly as elaborate as what she made for Toolie now. The next day Grandmother came over for dinner and handed her a small plastic bag. Mesi had torn into it, expecting the dress, and was disappointed to find only a square-foot piece of navy cotton.

"Grandmother, what's this?" she had asked.

"You wanted a dress, dear. And I will help you make one."

Miss Ama leaned against her walking stick. "You didn't get the answer you expected, but wasn't what your grandmother gave you even better?'

It was, thought Mesi. Because her grandmother taught her how to make a dress, she was able to make many dresses for Toolie instead of having just one. She was able to make that beautiful shawl for Kwasi. And now she was able to make enough money to go to school because Miss Makeena was buying the doll dresses from her.

Mesi had never thought of it that way. She looked at Miss Ama. "I'm glad she didn't give me what I asked for," Mesi said.

"God is good," Miss Ama said. "And he's been with you and your family this whole time. You didn't see him because you were looking somewhere else for him."

Suddenly everything seemed so clear to Mesi. Uncle Yorkoo said it was amazing Kojo survived the fire. Maybe God was the one who pulled Kojo out of the burning shack, who allowed them to travel into the city safely, who brought Miss Makeena down that market corridor that one wonderful day, and who—like Miss Makeena said—gave Mesi a wonderful talent. Maybe God had been more involved than she thought. And, in that moment, with all certainty she knew God truly had answered her prayer.

Miss Ama was still watching her. "Gold may not have been what you needed. As I recall, there are many robbers who watch for gold-diggers as they head back to their villages. Some are even killed so their gold can be stolen."

"So God may have been protecting Father—protecting us," Mesi said.

"Grace is God's gift to us even when we don't deserve it," Miss Ama said, gripping a wooden cross that hung from her neck. "And grace is like gold but better."

Mesi smiled. *Grace.* She'd heard the word before, but suddenly she was seeing it in a whole new light.

"There's something else about grace," Miss Ama said.

"What's that?" asked Mesi.

"It's buried in one place."

Mesi thought of gold buried in the earth.

Still holding the cross, Miss Ama said, "It is in Christ Jesus, God's only Son."

Mesi had heard the name Jesus. She knew he was special she just didn't know why—until now. "He is God's gold—the way God answers prayer?"

Miss Ama started trudging along the path again, and Mesi followed. "That, my dear, is correct."

Mesi felt proud inside, like she was wise . . . wise like a teacher.

In Step with the Times in Africa

© 2007 iStock/Peeter Viisimaa

Africa
Africa is a vast continent, diverse in terrain. Mountains, beaches, deserts, and jungles make up its beautiful landscape.

People
Africans are friendly people who live in rural villages or bustling cities.

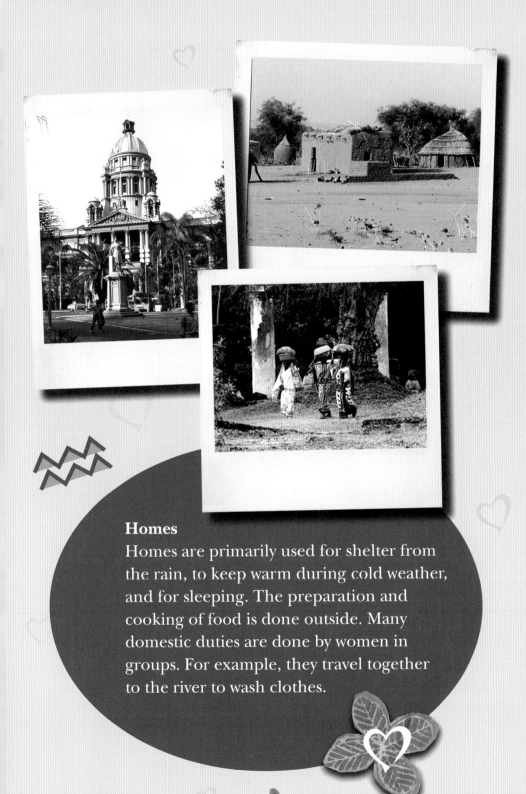

Homes

Homes are primarily used for shelter from the rain, to keep warm during cold weather, and for sleeping. The preparation and cooking of food is done outside. Many domestic duties are done by women in groups. For example, they travel together to the river to wash clothes.

Play

Dance, music, and mancala are favored activities throughout Africa. Mancala is a board game for two or more players. The wooden board consists of two rows of indentions, and the playing pieces are usually pebbles, seeds, shells, or even buttons. The object is to win your opponent's playing pieces, but the rules vary according to region.

Work
Industry in Africa is as diverse as the terrain. Fishing, farming, and mining are all important industries in Africa's economy.

Christianity

Christianity is a major religion in Africa.
Ethiopia has been a predominantly Christian
country since the fourteenth century.
Christian missionaries came to Africa in
the early nineteenth century, educating
Africans in the Bible, and serving in their
communities. When Africans converted to
Christianity they most often added a biblical
name to their African name.

A Real Life "Miss Ama"

Bathsheba's daughter, granddaughter, and great-granddaughter.

Although birth records weren't kept, Bathsheba Mugure Ngugi, was probably born in 1920 in Gatundu, Kenya. As a child, Bathsheba worked on the farm, helped her mother prepare and cook meals, and cared for her siblings. When she was fourteen, Salvation Army cadets came to her village to share the love of Jesus Christ. When she heard the gospel story, she felt God tug on her heart. She responded by kneeling in prayer and deciding to become a follower of Jesus Christ. She immediately liked the biblical name Bathsheba and took it as her Christian name. She met with Christians who taught her the Bible. But her mother and brothers weren't happy with her new faith. They believed girls didn't need to learn how to read and write, and girls certainly didn't need to go to church. When Bathsheba bought a dress for church, her brothers were so displeased they beat her and burned her dress. But this didn't stop Bathsheba from following Christ. With her only church dress burned, Bathsheba gathered *managu* leaves, a green vegetable that flourished in maize fields after the harvest, and sold them to buy another dress. Her family saw her dedication and devotion to Christ and realized that even if they beat her, she'd follow the Savior she'd grown to love.

At sixteen, Bathsheba met Joshua Ngugi, another African Christian, at a church fellowship. Bathsheba and Joshua eventually married, started a family, and then joined the Salvation Army to share the good news of God's grace. While attending the training, Bathsheba and Joshua lost two of their four children, one from measles and the other from an unknown cause. For Bathsheba and Joshua, the loss of these children was very painful as they trained to be ambassadors of Christ. Yet God blessed their devotion to him with more children. In all, Bathsheba gave birth to fourteen children—ten more than when she and Joshua joined the Salvation Army. Christian work for the Ngugi family was a family call to serve Christ. Bathsheba shared all the pastoral responsibilities with Joshua. She would preach on Sunday mornings, lead worship, help the sick, and perform funerals. But Bathsheba's first priority was always

to minister to her children because she wanted to see them come to the saving knowledge of Jesus Christ. Bathsheba's children, their children, and their children's children became living lights to the good news of God's grace in Christ Jesus, largely due to Bathsheba's choice as a young girl to embrace the God who tugged at her heart.

We celebrate the strength and wisdom that we have in Christ, so today and into the future we can become all that God has purposed.

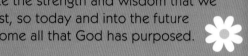
Girls 'n Grace 18" dolls have been beautifully sculpted by the renowned doll artist Dianna Effner.

International characters!

Discover an international community of Girls 'n Grace from Africa, the United Kingdom, India, Peru, and more!

I Can Through Christ!®

Girls 'n Grace Like Me! Collection

Choose a doll that looks like you!

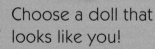

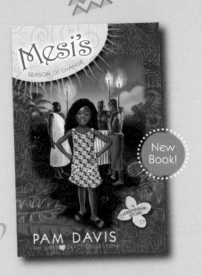

New Book!

Mesi's Season of Change: A Friendship Story

As the jungle rains diminish, a new friendship for Mesi grows– but this friendship has a secret. And Mesi must decide at what cost she will keep the secret and her new friend. Will she lose her best friend Kwasi? Anger her family? Or even bring destruction onto her entire village? Is offering grace worth the price?

Sydney Clair: A Girl 'n Grace in the 1960s

Sydney Clair Wilcox is a determined, curious ten-year-old trying to keep up with all the changes around her. The year is 1965. In the middle of the civil rights, women's rights, and environmental movements, Sydney discovers God's grace and how it makes her heart bloom.

Order online
www.GirlsnGrace.com

I Can Through Christ!®

Girls 'n Grace NIV New Testament

With an attractive cover to attract this generation of reader, Girls 'n Grace offers an NIV New Testament, the most widely accepted contemporary Bible translation today. The NIV New Testament was created to accurately and faithfully translate the original Greek, Hebrew, and Aramaic biblical texts into clearly understandable English.

Be sure and visit the Girls 'n Grace web site for games, quizzes, prizes, and more!

www.girlsngrace.com

In Touch With God in Africa

🌸 Was God at work in Mesi's life? _____

READ 2 CHRONICLES 16:9. What does this verse say about God's desire to work in your life? _____

_____

_____

🌸 Did God know Mesi's desire to go to school? _____

READ HEBREWS 4:13. Does God know your desires? Write some of your desires: _____

_____

_____

🌸 When Mesi's plans to provide for school failed, did that stop God's plans? _____

READ JEREMIAH 29:11. When you experience setbacks and failure will that stop God's plan for your life? _____

_____

_____

🌸 Did God love Mesi, even when she made a big mistake? _____

READ ROMANS 5:8. Does God love you even when you make mistakes?

_____

_____

Share this book and God's love with a friend,
so they can know the love and grace of God.